Poetic Licence

Martin Newell's poems appear weekly in the pages of
The Independent newspaper.

His previous publications include:

I Hank Marvinned	The Greyhound Press, 1991
Under Milk Float	The Greyhound Press, 1992
The Illegible Bachelor	Festival Books, 1996

The Illegible Bachelor and *Poetic Licence*
distributed by:
Turnaround
Unit 3
Olympia Trading Estate
Coburg Road
London N22 6TZ

Poetic Licence
also available mail order from:
J.L.M. & P.
75 Leverton Street
London NW5 2NX

Coming soon:
The Wild Man of Wivenhoe Festival Books / Jardine Press
Illustrated by James Dodds

Jardine Press
The Roundhouse, Lower Raydon
Hadleigh, Ipswich
Suffolk
IP7 5QN

Poetic Licence

Martin Newell

Jardine Press
1996

Thanks to John Walsh, Colin Hughes and Jane Lindsey.

Poetic Licence

Front cover detail from William Hogarth's *A Rake's Progress*
Printed by Progressive Printing, Leigh on Sea, Essex
Design and typography by Catherine Clark

ISBN 0 9525594 2 0

For
Miranda
and Wulf

Dear Reader

Herein are forty or so poems published in the pages of what Bill Bryson referred to as "Britain's liveliest quality daily." Since December of 1990, I've come up with well over 100 poems for The Independent's *Lyric Sheets* and for *Poetic Licence.* Since topical poems by definition, have a built-in obsolescence, the poems in this collection were the ones which to an extent have retained their currency.

Going typically against the grain, The Independent seem to prefer things which roughly rhyme, scan and are funny. This is just as well because although I can come up with work which has more gravitas, it is parody and satire which I probably do best. Some poetry readers prefer more serious stuff and I am occasionally damned by critics who say, "Not real poetry." Or even worse, "Yes. I think there is a place for light verse."

I enjoy writing the poems and I like sitting here in my attic in Essex, sniggering over my typewriter. Occasionally I've been asked to write a poem about a very difficult subject and have then been blithely informed that it's got to fill a page and can they have it in five hours please? This sort of fear is very good for a poet. People say, "It must be very hard." It's nowhere near as hard as going up and down a plank with a wheel-barrow full of hardcore, trying to fill a skip.

I'm very lucky. I get to pay the rent by doing something which I really like. I get letters from clergymen, housewives and meteorologists. I never lampoon in verse anybody whom I really hate. With the music page poems, when I write a jokey poem about some rockstar's excesses, I usually do it with the background of someone who has once been a fan and bought the records. I don't like being actually nasty. And anyway I might meet my subject one day.

The scariest commission I had was 1966 / 1996, the one about the England-Germany semi-final. Instead of my usual commission from Section Two, I was told that the Editor wanted me to write a poem for the front page.

"What?" I said. "You mean the main newspaper?"

"Yup." Came the reply. "That's right. The boys in long trousers."

I put the phone down and said something that rhymed with Truck Bee. Anyway they ran it. for a poet to get a front page is the equivalent of a pop star having a Number One hit single.

So do I hang out in London with a flute of sherry in my hand being witty with other poets? Er . . . no actually. I spend my spare time reading *Viz* and mucking about with dodgy rock musicians. That's all there is to say really.

Martin Newell / Essex / Autumn 1996

Contents

There Goes Non-Rhyming Garfunkel

Awkward on the record sleeves
Haircut wasn't right
Candyfloss-on-rugby-ball
Not a pretty sight
Known for singing very high
Caught the acting habit
Followed by a solo smash
Song about a rabbit.
Here a brief re-union
There a brand new start
Some reviewers say it's pop
Ah. But is it Art?

Linda McCartney's Pies

Paul McCartney in the kitchen
Helping Linda with her pies
Looked up from a finished pie-top
Gazed into his partner's eyes
Saying, "Since the Beatles finished,
Critics claim my tunes are limper.
Is this how my world has ended?
Not with a twang but a crimper?"

Two poems from the Independent Christmas issue 1993.

Badly Trained

Due to engine failure
Due to heavy rain
Due to creatures on the line
Regularly slain
By an earlier train

Due to one-day stoppage
Due to work restriction
Due to booklet, *Times of Trains*
Sold now under: FICTION
Due to dereliction

Due to broken goods train
Due to ancient stock
Due to frequent hand on
Panto-isolating cock
Major stumbling block

Due to frantic sell-off
Due to polling date
Due to foreign cowboys
Carving up the freight
Trains are running late

Due to previous franchise
Covertly decided
Due to engineering works
Frequently derided
Buses are provided

Due to a derailment
Due to wear and tear
Due to senior manager
Becoming millionaire
Trains may not be there.

The privatisation of the railways.

The Weekend Crusty

Ashes to ashes
Dust to dusty
Nathan is a weekend crusty
Anti-fashion
Fashion victim
Teams were chosen
No-one picked him
With the aid of Special Brew
You can be like Nathan too
Crack that tinny
Take a pew
This is what you have to do:

Don't talk posh
Learn to mosh
Soak your hair
In Go and Wash
Never rent
Only doss
Get yourself
A lurcher-cross
On a rope
Ditch the soap
Don't forget
To smoke some dope
Muddy boots
Filthy hands
Take to liking
Grungy bands
Five years on
When it's gone
TEFL course
Become a teacher
Then again
Grab a pen
Write a retrospective feature.

I Hank Marvinned

I Hank Marvinned
We all did
With cricket bats
In front of a mirror
In our bedrooms
After school
I Hank Marvinned
Quite regularly
My mother nearly caught me
What were you doing?
Nothing Mum
Cricket bat still warm
I Hank Marvinned
Unashamedly
On the bed sometimes
Standing up
I knew the dance steps
I thought I'd grow out of it
When I got married
But the other day
When she was out
They played Apache
On the radio
And I Hank Marvinned
In the living room
I straightened the place out
Afterwards
But somehow she found out
I'd been seen
You Hank Marvinned?
At your age?
She made me burn my cricket bat
And see a psychiatrist
I go to a special group now
Once a week
They give us all cricket bats
And black-framed spectacles
And we have to do it
Hank Marvin

In front of everybody
It's pathetic
Half a dozen men
In their late thirties
Cricket bats in hands
Spectacles on
Doing the dance steps
Grinning inanely
Shadows
Of our former selves.

The first Newell poem ever published in The Independent. From the verb; to Hankmarvin, meaning to emulate a guitar hero utilising some kind of sporting implement.

They Also Surf . . .

If Brian Wilson came from Clacton
And not the U.S.A.
He'd have a very different postcode
From Californ-I-Ay
You'd find it hard to imagine
The way it might have been
Had everycody gone surfin'
CO17.

Well East Coast girls are hip
I really dig those nylon flares
And the Southend girls
When they eat their chips
They knock me out when I'm down there
The Essex farmer's daughters
Wear their jodhpurs far too tight
And the Maldon girls
With the way they spit
At their boyfriends late at night
But I wish they all could be
Saffron Walden girls.

Well she hasn't got a car
And you can't rely on Eastern Region
And the Frinton Over 60s surfers
Had a very poor season
And they're rather short
Of happening bands
At the British Legion
But she'll have fun fun fun
Till her daddy takes the tea-bag away.

Beach Boys tributes poured in from Essex.

Sane, Good and Safe to Know

The poet's sane, it says so here
Forget the sex, the drugs, the beer
Bang goes my image and career
And this new study makes it clear
That malt does *less* than Milton can
To justify God's ways to man

I'll change my clothes this very day
And throw my silver boots away
And out will go my dandy shirts
And rakish hats but how it hurts
To pare my vast sartorial needs
Down to these brogues and Harris Tweeds

Despite Lord Byron and Rimbaud
I'm sane, I'm good, I'm *safe* to know
Perhaps you'd like to meet my wife?
We live a quiet suburban life
So bring your daughter round for tea
I guarantee she's safe with me

And healthy? God you'll never know.
I run, I cycle and I row
I do aerobics in the park
With fitness king, John Cooper Clarke
His body is a citadel
He partners me in squash as well

Myself, Attila, Hegley too
The sanest chaps you ever knew
Not locked in garrets being rude
Or drugged and dribbling in the nude
We're all of us on healthy food
To stave off any swings of mood

And Joolz the northern poetry muse
Despite those bangles and tattoos
Prevents herself from going barmy
When on tour by doing macrame
I'm sure she'd be the first to say
"No thanks." If strong drink came her way

Poets? Happy? Yes we are.
Life for us is caviar
Angst is banished to the shade
You hear that distant cavalcade?
It's merry poets out on parade.
But then of course, we're so well-paid.

But never trust that novelist.
He's sly, capricious, always pissed.
And taking drugs and breaking hearts
Or running off with seamy tarts
And so your poet's the ideal kit.
To ask around to baby-sit.

Poets - and take this as a rule
Will look into the Muse's pool
The better for a clearer head
And for the cleaner life they've led
Those Laudanum hallucinations
Only lead to aberrations

Take Coleridge. Please. An awful man.
I grant you he could rhyme and scan
But Kublai Khan as his best feat
Was far too long and incomplete
And we must tug a thankful forelock
To that drug-free man from Porlock

But what this study also said
And we must take the thing as read
Is that we poets are sometimes manic
Or depressed, but please don't panic
Tranquil sojourns in the bin
Mostly rein the problems in.

So fill my briar with ready-rub
But don't detain me in the pub
I'm not a blokish type of bloke
Is it my round? I'll get my cloak
I've got to do some yoga then
I have to be in bed by ten.

And call a poet up today
Invite one to your next soiree
Secure he won't be in your loo
Syringe in arm and turning blue
He's clean. He's safe. He's erudite
I hope you like him. *Poet Lite.*

A psychiatric study into the mental state of leading figures of literature suggested that poets were less prone to madness than other writers. The Independent's "Poet Laureate" was asked to assess his own state of mind.

The Singing Machine

They invented a singing computer
It could scat without missing a note
From Nirvana to Bing
It could croon, rock and swing
It was raunch with a digital throat

From the outset the thing had a fan-base
Which consisted of jaded technicians
Who could now do their jobs
Free of highly-strung yobs
And the equally bolshy musicians

While initially thought controversial
When it paired Pavarotti with whales
It was ambient-cool
Although strikingly cruel
To both bathroom and musical scales.

When the product became esoteric
After blending Ken Dodd with Madonna
A nod to the arts
Saw it storming the charts
With, "Domingo sings Hazel O'Connor"

As the thing lost its novelty value
And developed a problem with booze
To compound a cliche
It announced it was gay
In a deal with The News of the Screws

The machine went the way of all singers
And broke down on the eve of a tour
Then became rather odd
By discovering God
Having failed to regain its allure.

Radio Four's Today *programme, featured a computer capable of duplicating any singer's voice. Early experiments blended Pavarotti with whale-song. Obsolescence now beckons singers.*

The Republic 2000

(with apologies to A.A. Milne)

They're changing locks at Buckingham Palace
Christopher Robin went round with Alice
All the Queen's horses and all of her men
Found they belonged to themselves once again

They're opening gates at Buckingham Palace
While Christopher cruises around with Alice
He takes a swig from a bottle of beer
Saying, "Yo. It's totally excellent here."

They're housing the homeless at Windsor Castle
As part of the New Republican parcel
And all who assist with the moving of Liz
Will later be sorted for teas and fizz

With hustings located at Kensington Palace
Christopher Robin is voting with Alice
Not as peculiar as it once seemed.
"Jarvis For Prezza." The newspapers screamed.

They're chilling out at Buckingham Palace
Christopher Robin , The Prezza and Alice
Occasional calls for the Windsor Clan
Are greeted with, "Sorry. They moved out maan."

A poll of Sunday Independent readers indicated that if the monarchy were dissolved, Tony Benn would be favourite choice for President. Jarvis Cocker came second, with the Queen near the bottom of the list, only a few points above Mrs. Thatcher.

The Smurf Interview

(to the tune of The Smurfing Song)

Where are you all coming from?
All formats and C.D. ROM

Is this like The Pistols bash?
Yes but Smurfs make much more cash.

Where is Father Abraham?
Coming down off bad Edam.

What do Smurf songs signify?
Lack of taste at E.M.I.

What else do the Belgians sell?
Plastique Bertrand and Jacques Brel.

Are Smurf listeners mainly mugs?
Yes and ravers high on drugs

Who else thinks your songs are good?
David Icke and John Redwood.

When did you make this record?
Drying out in Betty Ford.

Who have you all worked with since?
David Bowie, Blur and Prince.

And a Smurf/Oasis hit?
Not since they sent us a writ.

We thought Smurfs were dead and done
When did that stop anyone?

La la lalalala lalalala
La la lalalala lalalala etc etc . . .

The Smurfs made a nineties comeback.

Rock Bottom

The art world reeled, the pop world spun
When Sunderland's most famous son
Afflicted by good taste no doubt
Announced he'd pulled his bottom out
The organisers in despair
Were sad he'd left it in the air
And since the stern would not be seen
They wondered how it might have been

They knew it was inflatable.
The rest was all debatable.
Magritte perhaps? With buttock face?
A pale pitted moon in space?
A horse-hair chair with razor slash?
Or Dali-esque with prop and 'tashe
Or would it take a modern view?
Formaldehyde then sawn in two?

What made the star abort his plans
And how will he console his fans?
His B-side won't be on display
Come autumn at the ICA
So has he left the thing too late?
Or are we left to speculate
That even Damien Hirst, (his friend)
Could not endorse his dorsal end?

Eurythmics star, Dave Stewart pulled his contribution out of an autumn ICA exhibition. It was to have been a giant inflatable model of his bottom.

The Great Beef Scare of '96

The minister announced the news
Reaction was volcanic:
All cows in byre
Must burn by fire
And media will be manic
And Everyman shall panic.

Then farmer shall be bought to book
With scientist and physician
For liege and lief
To place this beef
Beyond all foul suspicion
As popular nutrition.

And compensation shall be sought
When business has been bitten
By B.S.E.
Or C.J.D.
And letters will be written
Passed on to Leon Brittan.

Entreaties will be forwarded
And Europe, ever flighty
Will strike a pose
Of upturned nose
To act so high and mighty
About the beef in Blighty

But this is quite apart from it
The meat remains on table
Despite advice,
At half the price
The public seem quite able
To disregard the fable

Despite the B.S.E. scare, when Sainsbury's cut their beef prices by half, they sold out for the first time in 125 years.

The Downgrading of Hell

Hell hath no fire or brimstone pits
To scare us all out of our wits
No souls roast on infernal spits
The General Synod now admits

So sin away with less duress
Than checkmate in your Traveller's Chess
The Devil drives in casual dress
And Hell is merely nothingness

No smoking stairway leading down
No scorching buttocks frazzled brown
It's not the Hell of old renown
More like nil-nil at Ipswich Town

The version makes me more depressed
I liked the fiery image best
Do something wrong, it got redressed
A red-hot triton up your vest

A crumb remains to reimburse
The lonely sinner in his hearse
One's enemies have nothing worse
Than, "Go to Harlow." for a curse.

During the summer of 1996, The General Synod backed a Church of England report that Hell was a state of non-being rather than one of eternal torment.

First Cock-up Of Spring

Warm beer, village green and cricket
Spring comes dancing down the lane
In some pre-election thicket
Squawks the Redwood Bird's refrain

"Aarrk! The psychedelic sixties
Beatles, love-ins, liquid lights
I was there. Don't argue with me.
Grooving to the Barron Knights.

Lightning seeds now light my candle
And we've won the culture war
God bless Blur - but I like Handel"
Caws the clumsy bird once more.

Politicus Ignoramus
To employ its latin name
Has a call which is quite famous
Though it seldom sounds the same.

When it calls to younger voters
It attempts to ape their song
But its lack of sonic focus
Means it always gets it wrong.

Written during the week John Redwood M.P. endorsed Britpop, admitting that he was massively into the Barron Knights during the sixties.

The Brandy Of The Damned

This time of year an age ago
The muggy month of June
On London bus with first guitar
I heard one afternoon;
" Come on you scruffy bugger.
  And gissa bloody tune."

" Play us something that we know
  Something from the charts."
Travelling with instruments
This is how it starts
Brace yourself musician
- And welcome to The Arts.

In any heaving public house
On any grimy street
In all the damp rehearsal rooms
Where hairy yobbos meet
To struggle with a fledgling riff
And learn a basic beat.

Above the northern paper shops
Below the southern street
In dripping scuzzy cellars
Where drummers overheat
Provincial-oik-as-artist
The portrait is complete

The parents fret, employers moan
And thick and fast the flack
" You buck your ideas up my boy
  Or else you're for the sack.
  Music's not a proper job
  So push it to the back."

" You'll never make a living, son
By strumming that guitar
Get something you can fall back on
You won't get very far,
Drone, etcetera . . . good career . . .
And mortgage blah blah blah."

And thus the young musician leaves
Compounding parents fears
And serves a vast apprenticeship
Unpaid for many years
To join a rough and tumble
Which often ends in tears.

So this is where the rot sets in
And when you get the call
Your parents friends and partners
Are driven up the wall
Unless of course it happens
You're playing the Albert Hall.

The case is altered, naturally
And this is what they say:
" We always knew you'd do it.
Encouraged you to play . . ."
They buck you up, your mum and dad
But too late in the day.

For this is what musicians do
The feckless long-haired bums
They smoke and drink and fornicate
Until the morning comes
And then they try to change the world
With mere guitars and drums.

But in a case of boy-meets-girl
Or when your heart is broken
The prisoner in a tower somewhere
Inside you is awoken
And all the words which haunt you will
Be sung and rarely spoken

And all the riffs which rock the roofs
Of stadiums today
And all the stars who tread the boards
Began careers this way;
With boys and girls in backstreet rooms
Who had to learn to play

Above the northern paper shops
Below the southern street
In dripping scuzzy cellars
Where drummers overheat
Provincial-oik-as-artist
The portrait is complete.

I was asked to come up with a "really huge" poem for the National Music Festival. I remembered the words of George Bernard Shaw, who described music as "The Brandy of The Damned."

Tr'bute T'Rolf Herris

A kitten's fur-ball safely cleared
He helped but never interfered
That toothy grin and grizzled beard
You'd miss him if he disappeared
From Enimal Hosp'tl

From Sun Arise, he set the tone
Supremo of the Stylophone
And Woggle-board. A cornerstone
Of rock and roll he made his own:
Steerway T'Hivven.

It's surely due to oversight
The fact he's not been made a knight
And those cartoons were dynamite
All charcoal-sketched at speed of light
Ken yer giss what't izyet?

He pioneered the didgeridoo
A boon for any Crusty crew
God bless the gnarled old kangaroo
And now there's this new single due:
B'hemian Rhepsody.

Rolf Harris released a new single. It was his own version of Bohemian Rhapsody.

Judy And Her Partner

Judy is a victim
Needs to learn assertion
She should be disabled
In the P.C. version.
That's the way to do it.

Judy lives with Susan
Baby is their daughter
Mr. Punch has access
One weekend each quarter
That's the way to do it.

Mr. Punch the father
Should be far more caring
He could learn at workshops
Parenting IS sharing.
That's the way to do it.

By the way . . . that policeman,
Could be black and female
Punch would be arrested
Porno in his e-mail
That's the way to do it.

And that crocodile . . .
Makes the children edgy
Which brings us to the sausages
Shouldn't they be veggie?
That's the way to do it.

Mr. Punch is violent
And his dog is snappy
They should both be counselled
Forced to feel happy.
That's the way to do it.

Punch and Judy fell prey to Political Correctness. An American Punch and Judy person developed the first violence-free, p.c. show. It proved to be very popular.

Jackson versus Cocker 1997/8/9

The Jackson versus Cocker Case defied imagination
In the last years of the nineties when it ended in elation.
Leaving lawyers and accountants comatose for the duration
Having smashed existing records for the longest litigation.
It was televised and serialised and beamed out to a nation
Who were paralysed with gratitude and loss of concentration.

The foppish adversaries sat in hostile indignation
As their champions thrust or parried this or that denunciation
But undoubtedly the thing which most prolonged the situation
Was the hundred child witnesses thrown into the equation.
The presence of a chimpanzee caused further complication
While the crowded public gallery was moist with adoration

Parliament was dragged in when the case for mitigation
Called for Prescott, Blair and Bottomley to add corroboration.
But the single biggest factor which preceded culmination
Was the lawyers needing money and a threat of sequestration.
So the pettish two protagonists forgot their disputation
Then divided up the film fights and went out for a libation.

Jarvis Cocker, pranced around during Michael Jackson's showcase at the 1996 Brit Awards. A furious Jacko had Cocker arrested. Jackson threatened a law-suit but later backed off. As Cocker commented: "One of us has been in court for mucking about with kids . . . and it's not me."

Clapton At The Albert Hall (again)

As “Slowhand” in the Yardbirds
Then Cream, he could enthral
His wah-wah whacking Worship
Gave blues an overhaul
He didn’t dance around much
He hardly changed a string.
He made a classic, Layla
I bought the bloody thing.

Now several bearded teachers
Of geography and science
All want to watch him wielding
His wood and wire appliance.
And everytime it happens,
Their families say it’s odd
So many menopausal men
Still think of him as God.

And so for twelve nights only
A rough return to roots
The blues, as played by white men
In beige Armani suits.
Get corporate nostalgic,
Arrange to book a stall
And see how many trolls it takes
To fill the Albert Hall.

Neighbourhood Squat Scheme

Well-presented combat boot-a-terre
Three bed-semi. Vacant since recession
Open fires (in garden). Near to station.
Crowbar will secure quick occupation.

View today! Ideal for homeless couple.
Starter Squat. Southfacing. Off-road parking.
Double-glazing, cuts down sound of siren
Access via corrugated iron.

Well-proportioned Tudorbethan farm-house.
Breakfast room / five beds / two large receps.
Perfect halt for convoy during winter
Felling axe to door for easy-splinter.

Family home. May suit a hard-up couple.
Neg. Eq. victims. Children of school age.
Mid-Victorian. (As seen in depiction.)
Prettier in the viewing than eviction.

Mortgages foreclosed. Attractive houses.
Vacant now and many more to come.
Locks and chains being open to persuasion.
Homeless policy needs renovation.

A Squatting Estate Agents opened in Brighton.

Coz I Luvved It

Not Roxy, Bowie or T-Rex
But plumbers' mates in Rupert kecks
With pop songs for the refugee
From football ground and factory
The pilled-up beery boys like me.

We'd kick to death the working week
With Noddy Holder at his peak
And Friday lunchtime Lowenbrau
The foreman sneering at us now.
"And whatcha call that bloody row?"

And then much later, in disgrace
Drunk in the gutter, stars on face
Nineteen and witless, girlfriend fled
So dragged by mates and thrown on bed
The Slade songs roaring round my head

But Noddy Holder on Midweek?
My glam-rock haircut, layer and streak
Cut long ago reveals a brow
Where time has dragged a rusty plough
I'm several light years older now.

. . . and whatcha call that bloody row?

Twenty-five years ago, Slade first charted with Get Down And Get With It. *Noddy Holder featured on R4's* Midweek *at time of writing. The poet is a Slade fan.*

Adlestrop Retrieved

Bombastic, brash and over-prone
To shouting on his mobile phone
He's cancelling his three o'clock
Or booking tickets for Bangkok
So fellow travellers have no choice
But hear his self-important voice:
" I've godda window, Tuesday, noon.
 Yup. Abso-lootly. Speaktcha soon."
No sooner has he closed the thing,
His briefcase then begins to ring
And down it comes from off the rack.
" I'm breaking up. I'll call you back."
As fellow travellers wish he'd stow
His mobile phone where phones don't go
And so the pompous prat proceeds
From Paddington to Temple Meads.

But something just as vexing is,
The tiska-tiska-tiska fizz
Of Walkman-wearing younger chap
In baggy trews and baseball cap
Whose headphone-volume range can spill
From Very Loud to Louder Still
It's bad enough from town to town
But torture if the train breaks down
Had Edward Thomas known this lout
His poem would have not come out.
And all we'd know of Adlestrop
Was that the train had had to stop.
For if that bird had deigned to sing
This would have been the only thing
The poet heard close by and brisker:
"Tiska-tiska-tiska-tiska . . . . ."

Great Western Railways have made certain carriages on their daytime services, mobile phone-free zones. They have also barred personal stereos from end carriages.

Advice To The New Father (apologies to Lewis Carroll)

" You are old Father William," the new man said,
" And increasingly found in the wrong.
And while your wife lies in maternity bed
You stay in the pub all night long

" In my youth," Father William replied to the prig,
" They preferred the men out of the way
Of what the midwife would consider her 'gig.'
And none of us had any say."

" You are old," said the youth, "and you never assist
In the housework or give her support
And you watch the t.v. with a can in your fist
And she cooks as you wallow in sport."

" In my youth," said the sage," I worked hard as I could
And I brought home as much as was able
For years this arrangement was well-understood
And seemed to keep food on the table."

" You are old," said the youth, "and your credo's unsound
And you boast that you won't change a nappy
A marriage like this should have long run aground
Yet both of you seem fairly happy."

" In my youth," said the father, "I didn't dare dabble
And woman ruled kitchen and quilt
But now we're submerged in this Yank psychobabble
She's riddled with middle-class guilt."

" You are old," said the youth, "and I generally think
That you live a life absent of morals.
You sit there and wink as you hammer the drink
And you rest on your mildewed old laurels."

" I know," said the sage, "but a survey now states
That the women most likely to blub,
Are those who've been plagued by considerate mates
. . . Now f*** off and go to the pub."

‘A Shropshire Lad’: **LXIV The Missing Poem**

The idle lad on Wenlock Edge
Who hang-glides into trouble
May fall foul of a hawthorn hedge
And find himself bent double

For every athlete ends up dead
And life is endless rue
A hundred years ago I said
I’d die and now ’tis true

Oh I have worn my collars out
But London ones are stiffer
If Ludlow tailors seem in doubt
The hangman begs to differ

And twice a week the whole year through
I swore I’d not grow old
While sterling lads all died of ’flu
I merely caught a cold

With nooses here and firearms there
And poisoned pints of ale
We needs must jangle, how unfair
That I remained so hale

The lad who strode the Wrekin way
From Uricon knew grief
But now he keeps a house of clay
And oh, ’tis a relief

Sixty years after his death, A E Housman (1859-1936) has been memorialised in Poets’ Corner, Westminster Abbey.

← *New research revealed that pregnant women with attentive partners are likely to accrue a “caring debt,” leading to an increased chance of post-natal depression.*

The Sound Of A Bike

It's the sound of a bike
Which is part of the deal
And the well-oiled whirr
Of the sprocket and wheel
For the sound of a bike
Is distinctly genteel
And is holier now
Than the automobile

And the ching of the bell
On a bend in a lane
And the back-alley squeak
Of the brakes after rain
And the willow-herb wind
For the ghost of a train
Since the cinderpath track
Became cyclist's domain.

But the sound of a bike
Disappears without trace
In the madness of town
And the scrimmage for space
With the cut-up and curse
And the rage on the face
Of contestants engaged
In the circular race

For the sound of a bike
Has a subtler beat
In the click of its gears
And the crick of its seat
Than the harsh metal dirge
of a gridlocked elite
In their four-wheeled cells
On a five o'clock street

As part of the "Don't Choke Britain" Campaign, we held our first annual Bike-To-Work Day. A cyclist waxed lyrical.

Disastermind

It's sheer mental muscle
The egghead elite
A bluestocking groupie
Will kill for a seat
The portentious theme tune
Hangs black in the air
And caught in the spotlight
A totem . . . that chair

Take care, civil servant
To gird your i.q.
And firm up those facts
You were certain you knew
A crusty old viking
Adept with his tools,
The torturer Magnus
Will not suffer fools

Though confident once
With your specialist choice
A tic or a cough
And your tremulous voice
Betray you to millions
And there at the start
Six passes, wrong answers
Your game falls apart

An unemployed waitress
Compounds your defeat
Sixteen and no passes
The last round complete
You proffer a handshake
The shame undiminished
You blow it. They show it.
It's started. You're finished.

The TV programme, Mastermind began its 24th series.

A Breach of Essex

So me and Trace was well-annoyed
With Mr. Lilley. Want we Trace?
We bought this house in eighty-six
For forty K. Well on the case.
In them old days
Want we Trace?

And I was bloody coinin' it
Three motors and two videos
And d'you know what my house was worth
By '90? Ton-ten. As it goes.
The price just rose.
As it goes.

I voted for them four times round
So did Trace and her mate Sharon
My mates Russell, Kev and Warren
Their wives Heidi, Dawn and Karen
As it happens
So did Darren.

But would they get my vote this time?
Get a life. Not now I'm tryna
Pay the mortgage. Sold the motors
Last job? got the dustbin liner.
Trace is waitress
In a diner

Can't get dentists, hospitals are
Hopeless now. Don't even mention
Water, gas, electrics, buses.
Can't keep up the private pension
Never finished
My extension.

Estuary English spoken here.
We're satellite in town and dish
Peter Lilley don't be silly
Feelbad factor? Rampant . . . ish.
Fifth-time Tory?
Bet you wish.

Peter Lilley made an attempt to woo "Essex Man" by claiming that the conservatives were the true party of the working class. An Essex Man replied.

Downsized

We're pruning out dead wood
Recession-conscious now
We've rationalised the team
Less horses, faster plough.
New infrastructure needs
Have tightened up the show
The bottom line is this;
We'll have to let you go

We've hollowed out the log
And sorted wheat from chaff
The story didn't fit.
We cut your paragraph
Think of yourself as ex.
Or simply null and void
We've swept away the swarf
Arise Sir Unemployed.

We've re-assessed our needs
To run a lean machine
How many beans make five?
We ask a former bean.
We're tightening our belts
Re-tailoring the suit
As footwear rations stand
You'll find you've got the boot.

Our strategy is this;
You won't be coming back
But etiquette forbids
Us saying you've got the sack
So put another way
You've been reorganised
Redundancy-U-Got
But we prefer *"downsized."*

Wall Street's Duke of Downsizing, Stephen S. Roach, who for years had advocated mass redundancies in the name of efficiency, finally admitted that he'd got it wrong.

The Men Who Stole The Stars

Sirius. Andromeda.
Seemed less remote somehow
The pub garden astronomer
With pint in hand would now
Be pushed to see The Plough

So was it any wonder
As people spoke of Mars
And twittered psycho-actively
In pre-millennial bars
That someone stole the stars?

They floodlit church and castle
While all the country slept
And bathed the night in Skyglow
A colour so inept
That country lovers wept.

What? No more Ursa Minor?
And goodbye to Orion?
So shall the poet down his quill
With no stars to rely on.
And put a stupid tie on?

And will they grant a contract
To future lighting Czars?
As if the constellations
Were like unwanted cars
Then tow away the stars?

To the despair of poets, lovers and astronomers, Millennial plans to floodlight buildings threaten to banish the stars from the night sky. The U.K. Dark Skies Campaign regard Light Pollution as a serious problem.

A Very British Brothel

. . . So after consultations
And changing of the laws
The British standard Brothel
Threw open wide its doors
To tentative applause

The rooms were sparse and spotless
A bidet and a bed
The light above the chambers
Where clients would be led
Traditionally red.

Consumer-test inspections
Were now brought to the fore
A government committee,
The Ministry of Fworrr
Called twice a week or more.

These doughty politicians
Made sure that Sue or Brenda
Were tried and then found wanton
In stocking and suspender
For this was the agenda

The unemployed were given
A new incentive pack
Attractively entitled,
It took a simple tack.
PUT BRITAIN ON ITS BACK

" An interesting position?
Come join our friendly crew
For since you've entered Europe
It wants to enter you.
Please phone for interview."

During summer 1996, prostitution was mooted as a possible solution for unemployment. Later, several senior police chiefs recommended the legalisation of brothels.

Snogging In A Phone Box

In tea-rose red
The phone box then
Pretty on the green
With its cottage panes
We snogged in there
In our early teens
The tousled blonde
With smudged blue eyes
Who packed her boyfriend in
For me. Press Button B.
They don't come back

The oblong shape
Relieved by curves
Of bird-limed roof
The door was solid. Heavy
With its straps and handle
She phoned her friends
About the scandal.
That heady smell
Of cigarettes
And no regrets. Press Button B
They don't come back.

Late afternoon
Mid-autumn. Warm
The directory was torn
The half-term sun
Just she and I
And pennies for the guy
Then back at school
By now alone
She'd packed me in
Another phone. Press Button B.
They don't come back.

B.T. unveiled its new red phone box. There remain 15,000 of the old K6 design on British streets. Often mistaken for loos they are still an essential part of early courtship rituals.

Return Of The Station Master

A coal fire in his office
The fob watch in his pocket
The rigmarole of label-tying
With sisal-twine and docket
Which had to be respected
When parcels were collected

And well into the sixties
The best-kept village stations
The flower beds and livery
Receiving commendations.
Did station masters dream
In bottle-green and cream?

The breadth of Beeching's blunders
From Bedford to St Pancras
Was measured out in traffic cones
Container trucks and tankers.
While trains were scarcely faster
Without the station master

And when the vandal threatened
A way was found to foil it.
They placed surveillance cameras
And locked the station toilet
Then only found the key
If ticket staff were free

The newly-managed railways
Now find an old solution
Replace machines with human beings
And there's your revolution
Someone to take the flak
The staion master's back.

The much-missed station master was set to make a comeback. West Anglia Great Northern Railway announced their intention to restore masters to at least twenty stations before 1996 was out.

Keef

Feet on table
Fag in gob
The ultimate designer yob
A picture in the attic and
A blueprint for the older mob
Who slouched to school resentfully
Or hung around the cemetary
To scratch their love on mossy tombs
For tardy girls from coffee rooms.

The inkwell eyes and sullen stare
The lupine looks and bird's nest hair
Pervaded later rock and roll
The urchin dandy of its soul
And parents asked in disbelief:
"Who is that *Thing?"*
We called him Keef.

Guitarists spend their lives denying
His influence. Of course they're lying.
In posture, image, riff and hook.
They waste their time. He wrote the book.
And when he dies . . . and *if* he dies
The press will cluster round like flies
And every chorused voice will go:
"We told you so. We told you so."
And then they'll ask, in faint relief:
"What was that *Thing?"*

His name is Keef.

A 1996 poll of all age groups revealed that the most respected pop musician was Paul McCartney. The least respected pop musician was Keith Richards.

A Patient Writes .....

Doctors reek of glamour
Doctors ooze allure
Should they shtup their patients?
Why not? Sure!
Doctors must get lonely.
Look how hard they work.
Amorous encounters
Are the only perk.

Help your doctor help you
Lie down on the floor
Sigh: "Oh God I love you
        More. More. More.
Ring the B.M.A. up
That's the thing to do
Say your doctor's knackered
Then they send you two.

If a doctor calls you
Asks you how you are
Then proposes meeting
Later in a bar
Don't be sanctimonious
Change and comb your hair
Long as it's consensual
Nobody should care

Why do all these killjoys
Hurry to condemn?
It's because the doctor
Didn't fancy them
Do the patients want it?
Yes of course we do
Only thing that stalls us
Is the endless queue.

A debate was raging about the strict code of ethics forbidding consensual sex between doctors and patients. Why didn't they ask the patients?

The Iso-Bard

" Sweeping in from the Atlantic
  Packing in behind that low
  Showers bubbling - pretty beefy
  Many, right from the word, 'Go.'
  Morning mists burned off by sunlight
  Lingering on some north sea coasts . . ."
Nothing ever forged a forecast
Like the poetry of its hosts

Penny Tranter, Ian McCaskill
Kettley, Bacon, Giles and Lloyd
Temperatures quite academic
Lest the public be annoyed
Forecasts for less sheltered areas;
Cast no clout / don thermal vest
How they miss magnetic rainclouds
And the voice of Laurie West

Michael Fish, yet unforgiven
Garish tie, flamboyant jacket
Smarting still from 'eighty-seven
When the soft south caught a packet
Tossing coins, the luckier met men
Watch the spinning weather cocks
Suzanne Charlton, short of inches
Alan Ladd-like, mounts the box . . .

" Pretty chilly in that gale, with
  Gusts of up to forty-five
  Edging up to double figures
  When those lighter winds arrive . .
  Then tomorrow, clearing slowly
  Giving broken sunshine to
  Many west and central areas
  And that's it from Weatherview."

1966 / 1996

Oasis aren't the Beatles
And Blur are not the Kinks
As Double D. and Watneys Pale
Were not designer drinks
And ariels weren't dishes
And football songs weren't hip
As monocles and spikey hats
Weren't German football strip
And Mitchell wasn't Garnett
As Heath was not a fool
And Hamburg spawned the Mersey sound
As much as Liverpool
And Klinsmann isn't Haller
As Shearer isn't Hurst
And Ramsey was as much revered
As Venables is cursed

But mad old Tommy Tabloid
Still hammers at the hun
A powdered egg-bound xenophobe
Marooned in '41
He hears the grainy wireless blare
Across the sun-parched lawn
"4-2. 4-2." He must be true
To lion and unicorn
But younger generations
For whom his cant is meant
Will dress alike and dance alike
With or without consent
As sons of Thames or Tyneside
The Elbe, Rhine and Spree
Will only speak in Footballese
Upon the field of play

Published on the front page of The Independent 26th June 1996. The England-Germany football semi-final which ended in our defeat loomed. In the days leading up to the match, a wave of anti-German sentiment whipped up by the tabloids swept the country.

Sir Edward Heath

Teeth like terraced tombstones cut from chalkhills
A rictus like a radiator grille
His shoulder blades would judder
As he laughed and swung the rudder
Then steered us into "Yoorrp" for good or ill

" Bloody man, his three-day week, his power-cuts.
His plummy voice, his baton and his yacht"
The moans of protestation
From a candle-cadging nation
Who knew not then the outcome of the plot

Holed on union reefs, he upped his anchor
And sailed from Number Ten without applause
But when his new successor
Parked her handbag on the dresser
The "bloody man" would seem like Santa Claus

Edward Heath, "The Grocer" almost eighty
The Father of The House and decent chap
A voice of solid reason
In a xenophobic season
Despite the fact his spoken French is crap.

Townshend

Peter Dennis Blanford Townshend's
Sulky face stared out at me
Winter, nineteen sixty seven
From The Who Sell Out LP

Fifty shillings in old money
Proceeds from a paper round
Track one / side one, broken shards
Of backward psychedelic sound

Clanging daily from my bedroom
Twice before I ran to school
Sudden realisation dawning
That the Beatles weren't as cool

Like Hank Marvin's madder brother
Bird-man of the Goldhawk Road
Broken nails and Rickenbacker
Driving amps to overload

Heroes fit for boys in trouble
Spawn a tough and stubborn breed
So I struggled with a guitar
Til I made my fingers bleed

Peter Dennis Blanford Townshend
Gawky in his moddy togs
Never heard my schoolboy tributes
Ringing in the breaktime bogs

Never saw the windmill thrashings
Or the expert scissor-kicks
As the clumsy teen pretender
Dogged his Player's Number Six

Smoke On The Water

In music shops on Saturdays
You'll nearly always find
The faces of assistants there
Are prematurely lined
The reason for this ageing
Is repeated aural slaughter
By amateur guitarists
Playing *Smoke On The Water*
In kingdoms of the riffless
It's rated as the king
And once it's in the repertoire
They won't stop playing the thing
An iron-clad example
Of a riff which gives no quarter
The musical equivalent
Of solid brick and mortar
As popular as *Stairway*
But easier and shorter
An embolism - if you like
In rock and roll's aorta
It qualifies as music but
It's nothing like Cole Porter
It's Ritchie Blackmore's Frankenstein
Smoke On The Water

Ringo Starr

Ringo Starr Ringo Starr
Nodding dog in Beatles car
Dingle drummer, Ludwig kit
Kept the beat and sang a bit

Ringo Starr Ringo Starr
Mat to let him near guitar
Master of the tom-tom roll
Narrowly escaped the dole

Ringo Starr Ringo Starr
Clinking cowbells four each bar
Teenage memories coming back
Oh no. It's the Ringo track

Ringo Starr Ringo Starr
Better than Dave Clark by far
Never seemed to be as gear
Once he had his own career

Ringo Starr Ringo Starr
Did the drums on Drive My Car
Took a glammy second wife
Having had a hard day's life.

Richard Starkey - The 12 inch re-mix

Richard Starkey Richard Starkey
Never liked that drugs malarkey
Found the subject rather tawdry
Stuck with books by Reverend Awdry

National Anthem For Little England

John save our railway trains
Patch up our water mains
And submarines
Keep from the wrecking crew
Small shops and Doctor Who
Any thing that goes moo
And cheap baked beans.

This is our heritage
Names like Eileen and Reg
And warm flat beer
Lace curtains, cricket bats
Monogrammed toilet mats
Plays set in laundromats
And Clacton Pier

(There is a third verse but
no-one can remember it.)

With questions being raised in several of the papers about whether our national anthem should be changed. I was asked to come up with a modern alternative